SO-BZH-732

SPANIELS

LOYAL HUNTING COMPANIONS

BY TAMMY GAGNE

CONSULTANT:
ROBERT SANFORD
MEMBER
AMERICAN HUNTING DOG CLUB

CAPSTONE PRESS
a capstone imprint

Edge Books are published by Capstone Press,
1710 Roe Crest Drive, North Mankato, Minnesota 56003
www.capstonepub.com

Library of Congress Cataloging-in-Publication Data
Gagne, Tammy.
  Spaniels : loyal hunting companions / by Tammy Gagne.
     p. cm. — (Edge books. Hunting dogs)
  Includes bibliographical references and index.
  Summary: "Describes the history, care, and training of spaniels used for
hunting"—Provided by publisher.
  ISBN 978-1-4296-9907-5 (library binding)
  ISBN 978-1-62065-938-0 (paper over board)
  ISBN 978-1-4765-1550-2 (eBook PDF)
  1. Spaniels—Juvenile literature. I. Title.
  SF429.S7G34 2013
  636.752′4—dc23   2012027115

Editorial Credits
Angie Kaelberer, editor; Kyle Grenz, designer; Marcie Spence, media researcher;
Jennifer Walker, production specialist

Photo Credits
123RF: Juli Fergusen, 13; Alamy Images: Bob Jackson, 21, Realimage, 24 (left),
Stephen Loveridge, 10; Corbis: Dale Spartas, 29; Dreamstime: Ozgurphoto, 27;
Fotolia: CallallooAlexis, 12, Callalloo Candy, 7; Getty Images: David Tipling/Stone,
5; iStockphotos: CynthiaShepherd, 9, dageldog, back cover, 20, 22, 28, jamesbenet, 25,
jeffdalt, 17, kromeshnik, 4, LawrenceSawyer, 8, Robjem, 18, siloto, 1, urbancow, 19,
wpohldesign, 14; Shutterstock: cynoclub, 6, Lenkadan, front cover, Lori Carpenter,
15, Mackland, 24 (right), Nekrasov Andrey, 16, Pack-Shot, 11, Serdar Tibet, 26;
Wikipedia, 23

Printed in the United States of America in Stevens Point, Wisconsin.
092012   006937WZS13

TABLE OF CONTENTS

BORN TO
BIRD HUNT 4

MULTITALENTED
HUNTERS 10

A HUNTER
IN TRAINING 16

YOUR SPANIEL
AT HOME...................... 24

GLOSSARY 30

READ MORE....................31

INTERNET SITES 31

INDEX 32

CHAPTER 1

BORN TO BIRD HUNT

It is the moment the hunter and his spaniel have been training for all summer. A pheasant stands hidden in the brush as the spaniel slowly moves closer. The hunter cocks his gun, ready to fire. The spaniel speeds up, sending the bird high into the air.

English springer spaniels are among the best flushing breeds.

The hunter takes the shot, bringing down the pheasant. The spaniel quickly finds the bird and brings it back to the hunter. The spaniel's skill in **flushing** and retrieving the pheasant helps make the hunt a success.

flush—to force out of hiding

DOG OF SPAIN

Spaniels have been used to hunt birds and other small game for hundreds of years. It is believed that the breed began in Spain in the 1300s. The word spaniel comes from the French phrase *Chiens de l'Espanol,* which means "dog of Spain." But it was the British who mainly developed the breed.

Cocker spaniels were first bred to hunt birds called woodcocks.

DOG FACT

The Cavalier King Charles spaniel and the English toy spaniel are the smallest spaniel breeds. They are kept only as pets.

Sussex spaniels began in Sussex, England.

Until the 1800s, a spaniel litter often included pups of different sizes. By the end of the 1800s, people were breeding spaniels of the same size together. The largest dogs became springer spaniels, the medium-sized ones became Sussex spaniels, and the smallest became cocker spaniels. Spaniels came from England to the United States in the 1870s. James Watson and Clinton Wilmerding were two of the first American spaniel breeders. In 1881 the two men founded what is now called the American Cocker Spaniel Club.

HOW SPANIELS HUNT

Today many hunters consider spaniels to be the best all-around hunting dogs. The smallest of the **sporting dogs**, spaniels can easily move in and out of long grasses and thick brush. They crouch down as they sneak up on game. Next, they flush it out of the brush and into the air. Finally, they retrieve the fallen game after their owners shoot it. The soft spaniel mouth carries the game without damaging it.

sporting dog—a dog used to hunt game

Unlike some hunting breeds, spaniels work close by their owners as they flush game. This closeness continues in the home as well. Spaniels are both talented hunting dogs and loving pets.

SPANIEL SPECIALTIES

Breed	Best at Hunting
American Water Spaniel	ducks, grouse, pheasants, rabbits, quail
Boykin Spaniel	doves, ducks, grouse, pheasants, quail, turkeys
Clumber Spaniel	ducks, grouse, pheasants, rabbits
Cocker Spaniel	doves, Canada geese, ducks, pheasants, woodcocks
English Cocker Spaniel	ducks, grouse, hares, pheasants, woodcocks
English Springer Spaniel	ducks, grouse, pheasants, woodcocks
Field Spaniel	ducks, grouse, hares, pheasants
Irish Water Spaniel	ducks, geese
Sussex Spaniel	doves, partridges, pheasants, quail
Welsh Springer Spaniel	ducks, pheasants

CHAPTER 2

MULTITALENTED HUNTERS

Spaniel breeds are alike in many ways. These medium-sized dogs have short legs, long ears, and thick coats. Most spaniels are also friendly and intelligent. These qualities make spaniels easy to own and train. It also makes them great hunting companions for small game hunters.

Spaniels' legs and ears aid them in hunting and retrieving game.

A spaniel's short legs help it search through the underbrush when hunting. Its long ears hang low, trapping scents and directing them up toward the dog's nose. A spaniel's thick, wavy coat keeps the dog warm and dry in most types of weather.

CHOOSING A HUNTING SPANIEL

The best place to find a spaniel puppy is from a breeder with a good reputation. Ask other hunters or contact a hunting dog club to get the names of good breeders. When you visit a breeder, ask to see where the dogs are kept and to meet the puppy's parents.

Your breeder can help you find the best spaniel for the kind of hunting you want to do. Pups that grow up to be talented hunters often have parents who have

already proven themselves in the field. Spaniels often show signs of **birdiness** when they are just a few weeks old.

birdiness—natural talent for bird hunting

SPANIEL BREEDS

Prey drive runs deep in spaniels. Even dogs that aren't trained to hunt have a natural **instinct** for the sport. It isn't unusual for a pet spaniel to chase birds in the backyard.

Each breed brings its own set of skills to the hunt. Cocker spaniels, English cockers, and English springers are known for flushing game from thick cover. English springers are especially fast, probably because they have the longest legs of all spaniels.

The Clumber is the largest spaniel breed.

It isn't a surprise that Clumber spaniels, field spaniels, and Sussex spaniels aren't as fast as other spaniels. They have the shortest legs. But they are talented. As they hunt, they seem to cover every inch of the hunting area.

instinct—behavior that is natural rather than learned

The Boykin spaniel is nicknamed the swamp poodle.

Both the American water spaniel and the Boykin spaniel are skilled at hunting in the water. The Irish water spaniel and the Welsh springer spaniel are strong hunters both on land and in water. The Welsh springer is also a good retriever.

For many years the Brittany was called the Brittany spaniel. But its hunting style is more like that of the pointing breeds. In 1982 the American Kennel Club (AKC) dropped the spaniel from its name for this reason.

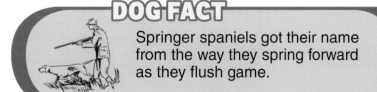

DOG FACT

Springer spaniels got their name from the way they spring forward as they flush game.

SPANIEL TAILS

Everything about spaniels makes them perfect for hunting, except for one thing. Their long tails can be a problem in the field. A dog can become injured if its tail gets caught in the brush. This is why most hunting spaniel breeds have docked tails. Shortly after pups are born, breeders snip off all but a few inches of their tails.

Most spaniels have docked tails.

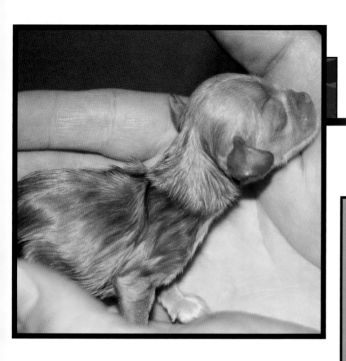

A puppy's tail is docked shortly after it is born.

Docking isn't painful as long as it's done when the puppy is 3 to 5 days old. The nerves in the tail aren't fully developed at this time. Even so, many people think that tail docking is cruel. It is illegal in many European countries, but exceptions are sometimes made for hunting dogs.

Water Hunters

All spaniel breeds can be trained to hunt and retrieve ducks and other waterfowl. But two breeds are especially known for this skill—the Irish water spaniel and the American water spaniel.

The curly-coated Irish water spaniel is the tallest spaniel breed. It began in Europe around the 700s. The modern breed can be traced to a spaniel named Boatswain, which lived in Ireland during the 1830s. American breeders in Wisconsin used Irish water spaniels and curly-coated retrievers to develop the American water spaniel in the mid-1800s. This breed is the rarest of the spaniels, with only about 3,000 dogs worldwide.

15

CHAPTER 3

A HUNTER IN TRAINING

You can start training your spaniel puppy the day you bring it home. Keep training periods short during the first three months, though. Younger pups learn best from short, frequent sessions. Make training fun to keep your pup's attention. Think about how you learn best. If your teacher makes a school assignment enjoyable, it is easier to do well.

Get your dog used to the scent of the birds it will be hunting.

Before hunter training begins, teach your spaniel some basic **obedience** commands. Hunting dogs don't wear leashes in the field. They must obey their owners' voice commands from at least 10 to 20 yards (9 to 18 meters) away. Basic obedience commands include sit, stay, and come. Following these commands helps keep your spaniel safe on a hunt.

Dog treats can help in training your spaniel.

You can use dog treats as training rewards. The best reward of all, though, is praise. Never yell at or hit your dog for doing something wrong or being slow to learn. When your puppy knows you are pleased with it, it's more likely to do what you want.

obedience—following rules and commands

HUNTING COMMANDS

Once your pup understands basic commands, you can start hunter training. This stage combines practicing old commands with learning new ones. One of the most important commands a spaniel must learn is "hup." When an owner says this, the dog should sit and stay. Use the command "gone away" to teach a pup to ignore a bird that has flown away.

Some hunters teach their spaniels whistle commands. Two quick whistles, or pips, tell a dog to turn in the opposite direction. A long whistle means the same thing as hup.

"Hup" tells a dog to stop and focus on its owner.

QUARTERING AND DUMMY TRAINING

One of the most difficult parts of training is teaching your spaniel to **quarter**. Quartering makes sure that the dog covers as much hunting ground as possible. It's a bit like the way search and rescue work is performed. Take your dog to an open area. Walk ahead of it, and then extend your arm straight to the right, while calling or blowing on a whistle for your dog to come to you. Then walk forward and move to the left, extending your arm to that direction while calling for your dog. Over time, perform the training on larger areas of ground until your dog knows how to move swiftly in a zigzag pattern.

Some dogs work in a wide circle until they see or hear the game. They then start quartering to narrow down the game's location.

quarter—to move in a zigzag, boxlike pattern

Dummies help spaniels learn to retrieve.

Around this time you can begin using a training **dummy** to teach your dog to retrieve game. The dummy should be about the same size and weight of a bird the dog will be hunting in the future. Throw the dummy when you are training with your spaniel. When your dog brings the dummy to you, say "give" as you gently remove the dummy from its mouth. Your dog will soon learn that it needs to bring and release the game to you.

DOG FACT

Some owners attach feathers to dummies to make them look and smell more like real birds.

dummy—a training toy used as a substitute for a bird

THE FIRST HUNT

On its first hunting trip, your spaniel may have a hard time following commands in a new place. Try training your spaniel in a similar setting before the first actual hunt. Your dog will be less likely to be distracted by unusual sounds and smells.

Keeping your spaniel close on its first hunt can be a challenge. Many dogs want to run too far ahead of their owners once they get into the field. To prevent this, try moving into the direction of the wind. This encourages the spaniel to quarter in a smaller area. The closer your dog is to you, the more control you will have over it. This is especially true with younger dogs.

Spaniels must learn to release game to their owners.

One of the best ways to teach a spaniel to hunt is by example. Younger spaniels can tag along on hunts with more experienced gun dogs. Some older spaniels will even allow a younger pup to help carry the game.

HUNTING STYLES

Although spaniels hunt in similar ways, every breed is a little different. For example, the American water spaniel is known for being cautious around strangers. It probably won't learn as easily from a professional trainer as it will from its owner.

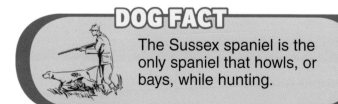

DOG FACT

The Sussex spaniel is the only spaniel that howls, or bays, while hunting.

American
water spaniel

The Sussex spaniel often learns at a slightly slower pace than other spaniels. Sussex owners should break down tougher tasks such as quartering into several small steps. Even dogs of the same breed can be a little different from one another. A training method that works for one dog may not work for another.

Gun Training

Even the best-trained dog won't make a good hunting companion if it is gun-shy. Before your dog's first hunt, use everyday objects to get it used to loud noises. Clanging two cooking pots together can help a pup understand that loud noises won't hurt it. Making this noise each night just before dinner can show it that loud sounds can even come with rewards.

CHAPTER 4

YOUR SPANIEL AT HOME

Training a hunting spaniel takes time, effort, and lots of patience. Both gun dogs and their owners need regular breaks. After a day of hunting, spend time relaxing and playing with your dog. A happy spaniel that has a strong bond with its owner will work even harder to please its master in the field.

Spaniels are active dogs. They need regular exercise every day, not just during hunting season. Take your spaniel for a walk at least once or twice a day. Spaniels also do well in dog sports competitions such as agility and flyball.

Agility involves racing through obstacles.

GROOMING

Spaniels' long coats need to be brushed about twice a week to keep the hair from tangling and forming mats. Most spaniels have long hair called feathers on the backs of their legs. Use a fine-toothed comb daily on the feathers and the long hair behind the ears. When your dog has been out hunting or training, check its coat for burrs and ticks and remove them right away.

You can bathe your spaniel outdoors in warm weather.

Unless your spaniel gets into something very messy, it can go several months between baths. Spaniels have natural oils in their skin that make their coats resistant to water. Bathing them too often can remove these oils.

HEALTHY HUNTERS

All dogs need regular veterinary care. Take your spaniel to the vet at least once a year for a checkup and any needed vaccinations. Your vet will also supply you with medicine that prevents fleas, ticks, and mosquitoes from spreading diseases to your dog.

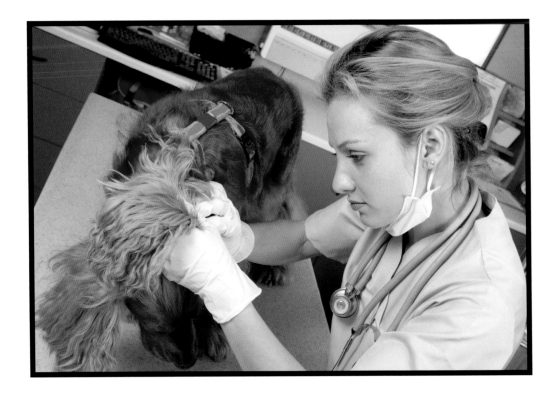

Every dog breed can have health problems. For spaniels, these include **allergies**, ear infections, and eye and hip problems.

allergy—sensitivity to something in the environment

Most allergies in dogs are food related. **Hypoallergenic** dog foods are available to help with this problem. These foods are made without common allergy-causing ingredients, such as grain.

Feed your spaniel once or twice each day.

Spaniels often hunt in water. Water can become trapped in your spaniel's ear canal and cause an infection. Check your spaniel's ears after every hunt and clean them at least once a week.

hypoallergenic—having a quality that reduces or stops allergic reactions

Check your spaniel's eyes after each hunt or training session in the field. Many spaniel breeds have large eyes that can be injured by sharp branches. Another common eye problem in spaniels is **cataracts**. Cataracts can cause blindness, but surgery can usually correct the problem.

All spaniel breeds can develop hip dysplasia.

Hip **dysplasia** is found in all spaniel breeds. Dogs with this condition have problems standing and walking, especially as they grow older. When choosing your spaniel puppy, ask the breeder if the dog's parents have been tested and cleared for hip dysplasia.

Owning a hunting spaniel can be a lot of fun, but it also requires regular training and care. The rewards for these efforts can be big, though. As long as you are willing to do your part, you will end up with a useful hunting companion and a beloved four-legged friend.

cataract—a white film on the lens of the eye

dysplasia—a condition in which an animal's elbow or hip joints do not fit together properly

GLOSSARY

allergy (A-luhr-jee)—a sensitivity to something in the environment such as dust, pollen, or food

birdiness (BURD-ee-ness)—a dog's natural talent for bird hunting

cataract (KAT-uh-rakt)—a white film on the lens of the eye

dummy (DUHM-ee)—a training toy used as a substitute for a bird

dysplasia (dis-PLAY-zhah)—a condition in which an animal's elbow or hip joints do not fit together properly

flush (FLUHSH)—to force out of hiding

hypoallergenic (hye-poh-a-luhr-JEN-ik)—having a quality that reduces or stops allergic reactions

instinct (IN-stingkt)—behavior that is natural rather than learned

obedience (oh-BEE-dee-uhns)—following rules and commands

quarter (KWAWR-ter)—to move in a zigzag, boxlike pattern

sporting dog (SPORT-ing DAWG)—a dog used to hunt game

READ MORE

Gagne, Tammy. *The English Springer Spaniel.* Terra-Nova: Discover a Whole New World of Dogs. Neptune City, N.J.: T.F.H. Publications, 2009.

Martin, Michael. *Pheasant Hunting.* The Great Outdoors. Mankato, Minn.: Capstone Press, 2008.

Zuchora-Walske, Christine. *Setters: Loyal Hunting Companions.* Hunting Dogs. North Mankato, Minn.: Capstone Press, 2013.

INTERNET SITES

FactHound offers a safe, fun way to find Internet sites related to this book. All of the sites on FactHound have been researched by our staff.

Here's all you do:

Visit *www.facthound.com*

Type in this code: 9781429699075

 Check out projects, games and lots more at **www.capstonekids.com**

INDEX

appearance, 10, 12, 14

birdiness, 11

breeders, 7, 14, 28

breeds
    American water, 8, 9, 13, 15, 22
    Boykin, 8, 9, 13
    Brittany, 13
    Clumber, 9, 12
    cocker, 7, 9, 12
    English cocker, 9, 12
    English springer, 7, 9, 12, 13
    field, 9, 12
    Irish water, 9, 13, 15
    Sussex, 7, 9, 12, 14, 23
    Welsh springer, 9, 13

care
    feeding, 27
    grooming, 25
    vaccinations, 26
    veterinarian visits, 26

clubs, 7, 11, 13

commands, 17, 18, 21

competitions, 24

dummies, 20

exercise, 24

feathers, 25

flushing, 5, 8, 9, 13

game, 6, 8, 9, 10, 13, 19, 20, 22

health issues, 26–27, 28

history, 6–7

puppies, 7, 11, 14, 15, 16–17, 18,
    22, 23, 28

tails, 14–15

temperament, 9, 10

training
    basic, 17, 18
    gun, 23
    quartering, 19, 21, 23
    retrieving, 5, 8, 13, 15, 20